D0646923

SPACE

Ting and Neil Morris

Illustrated by Raymond Turvey

SEA-TO-SEA
Mankato Collingwood London

⚡!⚡ This symbol appears on
some pages throughout
this book. It indicates
that adult supervision
is advisable for that
activity.

This edition first published in 2007 by
Sea-to-Sea Publications
1980 Lookout Drive
North Mankato
Minnesota 56003

Library of Congress Cataloging-in-Publication Data
Morris, Ting.
  Space / by Ting and Neil Morris ; illustrated by Raymond Turvey.– Rev. ed.
    p. cm -- (Sticky fingers)
  Includes index.
  1. Astronautics--Juvenile literature. 2. Outer space--Juvenile literature. 3.
Handicraft--Juvenile literature. [1. Astronautics. 2. Outer space. 3. Handicraft.] I.
Morris, Neil, 1946- II. Turvey, Raymond, ill. III. Title.

TL793.M657 2006
629.4--dc22

                                                          2005058147

9 8 7 6 5 4 3 2

Published by arrangement with the Watts Publishing Group Ltd, London

Editor: Hazel Poole
Consultant: Simone Lefolii
Designer: Sally Boothroyd
Photography: John Butcher
Artwork: Raymond Turvey
Models: Emma Morris
Picture research: Juliet Duff

Contents

Introduction

In this book you can learn about space both by reading about it and by having fun with craft activities. The information in the fact boxes will tell you about our planet, Earth, the other planets in the solar system, and other stars and galaxies in the universe. You will also learn about traveling in space, possible space colonies of the future, and the search for alien life.

At the end of the book is an illustration of our solar system, with information on our own star — the sun. There is also a list of books to read, places to visit, and organizations to contact if you want to find out more.

Now you can get ready to get your fingers sticky — making space models as you read all about the universe!

Equipment and material

The projects in this book provide an introduction to the use of different art and craft media, and need little adult help. Most of the objects are made with throwaway household "junk" such as boxes, plastic bottles and containers, newspaper, and fabric remnants. Paints, brushes, glues, and modeling materials will have to be bought, but if stored correctly will last for a long time and for many more craft activities.

In this book the following materials are used:

balloons (round)
bottle tops
bowls
brushes (for glue and paint)
buttons
cardboard boxes (large and small)
cardboard lids
cardboard tubes (large and small)
cereal boxes
chocolate box tray
cookie sheet
cooking oil
cotton thread
craft knife
crayons
cutting board
die
dishwashing liquid
egg cartons
felt (gray)
felt-tip pens
flour
flowerpot (small, plastic)
foam pieces
foil (colored, gold and silver)
foil dishes

foil stars (with gummed or adhesive backs)
fork
Fun-Tak
glitter
glue (water-based PVA, which can be used for thickening paint and as a varnish; strong glue such as UHU for sticking plastic, metal, and fabric; glue stick)
jar (for mixing paint and paste)
marker pen (black)
matchboxes
measuring cup
modeling clay
nails
needle
nylon thread
packaging material
paint (powder, ready-mixed, poster, and acrylic paints)
paper (white; oak tag; corrugated paper; crêpe paper; cardboard; tissue paper; tracing paper; newspaper; construction paper)
paper clips
pencils

plastic bottles (large)
reflector strips
rubber boots
rubber gloves
rubber tubing
ruler
salt
scissors
screws
spools (from thread)
spoon
springs
steel wool soap pad
straws (bendable)
string
Styrofoam
tape (transparent tape; masking tape; silver tape)
toothpaste caps
toothpicks
trash can liner (black)
varnish (PVA mixed with cold water)
washers
water
wiffle ball (plastic ball with holes in it)
wire coat hanger
yoghurt containers

Our Planet

Here's a good way to make a model of our planet — Earth.

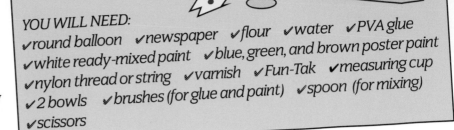

YOU WILL NEED:
- ✓round balloon ✓newspaper ✓flour ✓water ✓PVA glue
- ✓white ready-mixed paint ✓blue, green, and brown poster paint
- ✓nylon thread or string ✓varnish ✓Fun-Tak ✓measuring cup
- ✓2 bowls ✓brushes (for glue and paint) ✓spoon (for mixing)
- ✓scissors

1 First tear some newspaper into narrow strips about 1 inch (2 cm) wide.

2 In a large bowl, make some papier-mâché paste by mixing one cup of flour with two cups of water until the mixture is smooth and creamy.

3 Blow up a round balloon and put it in a bowl to hold it steady while you are working. Coat each strip of newspaper with paste. Pull each strip between your finger and thumb to remove any lumps. Cover the balloon with one layer of strips in one direction, and then a second layer in the other direction. Smooth down all the strips with your fingers. Make at least four layers of papier-mâché strips, and then leave to dry for a couple of days.

4 Pierce a small hole in the top of the planet. Knot the end of a piece of nylon thread or string and push the knot into the hole. Secure it with PVA glue and glued paper squares. When the glue is dry, paint the planet with a thick layer of white paint.

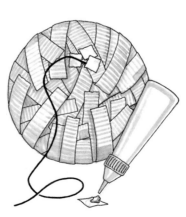

Earth

The earth moves on a path around the sun, along with the other planets in the solar system. In some ways it is no different from other planets, which are huge balls of rock, metal, or gas that do not give out any light of their own. Like Mercury, Venus, and Mars, Earth is made mainly of rock. It has a metal core at the center and is surrounded by an atmosphere of gas. Most scientists believe that the sun and the planets were formed about 4,600 million years ago from a cloud of dust and gas in space. Earth is about 9.3 million miles (150 million km) away from the sun. This particular distance is just right for the amount of light and warmth needed for water and air on Earth. Animals and plant need these to live. Most of the earth's surface is covered by seas and oceans. Viewed from space, our home is a blue planet covered with swirling white clouds.

5 When the white paint is dry, paint the planet's surface like the photograph of Earth as it looks from a satellite in space. Paint blue sea, green and brown land, and white polar regions.

6 Let your planet Earth dry. Then you can varnish it and ask an adult to hang it from the ceiling with Fun-Tak.

Space city

YOU WILL NEED:
- ✓ base of a large cardboard box ✓ plastic packaging
- ✓ cardboard tubes ✓ round plastic lids ✓ plastic bottles
- ✓ small balls ✓ yogurt containers ✓ cans
- ✓ white ready-mixed paint ✓ silver and gold poster paint
- ✓ PVA glue ✓ strong glue (UHU) ✓ Styrofoam
- ✓ cardboard ✓ brushes (for glue and paint) ✓ toothpick
- ✓ scissors ✓ silver foil

1 Before you start constructing your space city, look carefully at your collection of junk materials and containers. Choose those with the best futuristic shape. Decide on a layout for the city before gluing your buildings onto the base of a large cardboard box. You may want to adapt the following suggestions according to your own ideas and materials.

2 Have a grown-up cut some large plastic bottles in half to use as domes for people to live in. Some soda or juice bottles have an extra plastic base. If you pull this base off, you will find a domed shape underneath. You could arrange bits of plastic packaging and yogurt containers around the domes.

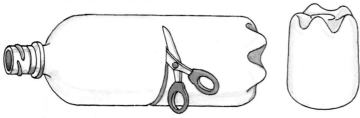

4 Ask an adult to cut off the top of a large plastic bottle and cover it with foil to make a large radio telescope. Antennas and satellite dishes can be made from round cardboard lids and foil dishes.

3 Cover cardboard tubes and cans with silver foil to make a network of passages connecting the buildings. Fit a small ball on top of a tube to make a space tower.

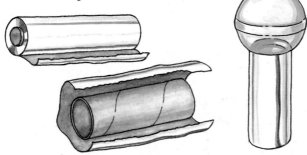

5 Glue all these constructions to the cardboard base. Then mix some white ready-mixed paint with PVA glue and paint the base and some of the constructions with this mixture. When this is dry, which will take one or two hours, add details with gold and silver paint.

Turn to pages 16 and 17 to see how to make lunar buggys.

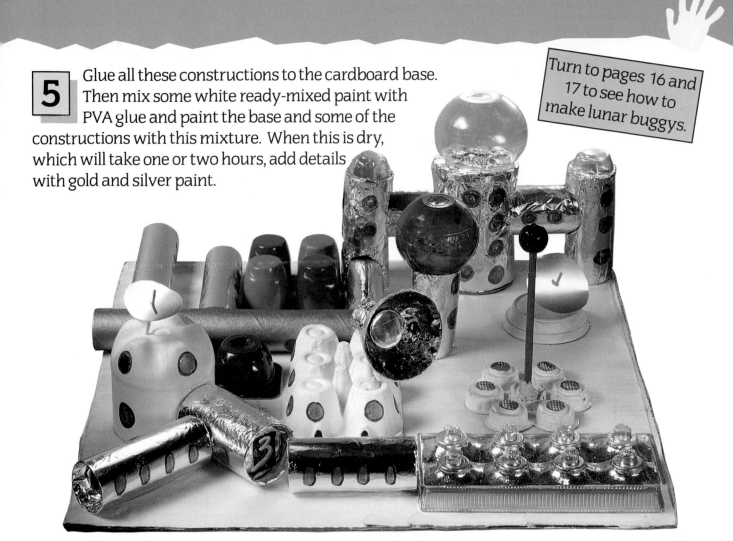

Colonies in space

In the future, people might live in space colonies orbiting the earth, on the Moon or on other planets. The next place astronauts are likely to visit is Mars. It will take at least six months for spacecraft to get there, but it should be safe to land on. The unmanned *Viking 1* spacecraft landed on the surface of Mars in 1976 and took photographs of the Martian landscape *(left)*. It is a very cold and windy planet, with a thin atmosphere of carbon dioxide. People would have to live inside protective buildings filled with air. They would also have to wear space suits outside. Life in a space city could be similar to life on Earth. Mars has a day and night similar to that on earth.

Astronaut

Get ready to travel in space.

YOU WILL NEED:
- cardboard box ✓gray felt
- ✓two thread spools ✓string
- ✓PVA glue ✓toothpaste caps
- ✓two large plastic bottles
- ✓silver foil ✓rubber boots
- ✓scissors ✓rubber gloves
- ✓bottle tops ✓reflector strips
- ✓two cereal boxes ✓tape
- ✓rubber tubing ✓brush ✓lid
- ✓bendable straw

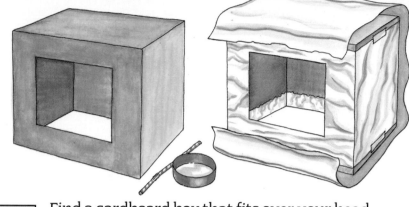

1 Find a cardboard box that fits over your head comfortably. Ask an adult to cut out a large rectangular hole at the front. Then cover the helmet with silver foil. Glue down the edges. A foil-covered lid with a bendable straw taped to it makes an antenna.

2 To make a "life-support system," first cut two straps out of felt, long enough to fit over your shoulders. Tape them to the cereal boxes.

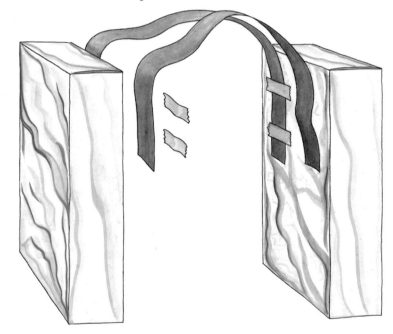

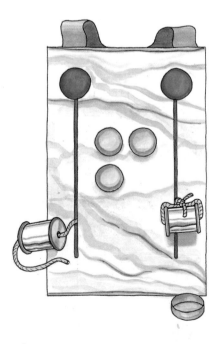

3 Cover the boxes with silver foil. Carefully cut two slots in the control panel worn at the front. Thread a piece of string through the slots and tie a thread spool to each end. Now you have a control that slides up and down in each slot. Glue bottle tops and caps onto the panel for more controls.

4 For the oxygen tanks, cover two large plastic bottles with silver foil. Connect the bottles with foil-covered tubing. Tape them onto the backpack.

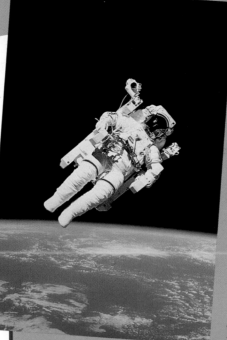

Space suits

When astronauts leave the safety of their spacecraft, they wear a space suit. This protects them from dangerous radiation and speeding dust, and supplies them with air to breathe. A space suit is made up of many layers, to keep out the cold of space and the heat of the sun. One of the inner layers controls the astronaut's temperature by passing water through plastic tubes. The helmet has a dark visor to protect the eyes from strong sunlight, and earphones and a microphone for talking to other astronauts or to ground control. The backpack holds enough air and water for the astronaut to go on a space walk for several hours. To go farther from the spacecraft, an astronaut can put on a special backpack called a Manned Maneuvering Unit (or MMU). This has small jets that allow the astronaut to move through space in any direction.

5 Attach reflector strips to a pair of rubber boots and rubber gloves.

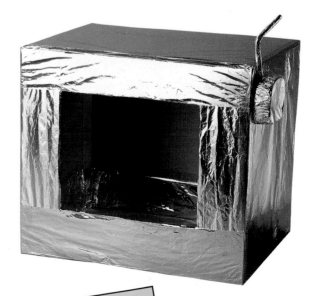

Now you are ready for the countdown!

Solar Mobile

YOU WILL NEED:
- ✓ newspaper ✓ thin white paper
- ✓ masking tape ✓ foil tape
- ✓ transparent tape ✓ PVA glue
- ✓ nylon thread ✓ poster paints
- ✓ water ✓ ruler ✓ compass
- ✓ pencil ✓ scissors ✓ cardboard
- ✓ wire coathanger

This chart gives the size and color of each model planet. The smaller planets are roughly to scale with each other, as are the larger planets, but we have had to alter the scale overall. Our Jupiter is 15 times bigger than Pluto. In reality it is over 62 times bigger, as you can see from the chart on page 29.

planet	model diameter		color
	(inches)	(cm)	
Mercury	1¹/₂	4	gray
Venus	3¹/₂	9	yellow-white
Earth	4	10	blue
Mars	2	5	red
Jupiter	12	30	orange
Saturn	10	25	yellow
Uranus	8	20	green-blue
Neptune	7	18	blue
Pluto	1	2	gray

1 Scrunch some newspaper into a ball, slightly smaller than the model diameter. (For example, 1 inch [3 cm] for Mercury), and secure it with masking tape.

2 Tear some newspaper into narrow strips. Dip the strips in PVA glue diluted one part glue to one part cold water. Cover the ball evenly with the strips to make a smooth surface.

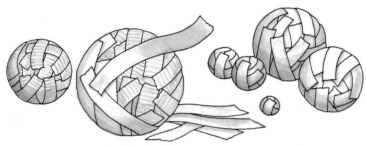

3 Now cover the ball with glued white paper strips until the newsprint can no longer be seen. Follow steps one through three for all nine planets.

4 Let the models dry for at least one day before painting them in their basic planet colors.

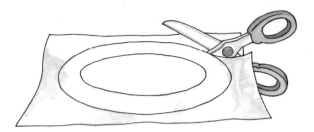

5 To make Saturn's rings, draw a 10 inch (27 cm) wide circle on some cardboard. Then draw a 12 inch (30 cm) circle around it. Cut out the inner circle and then cut around the outer circle. Color the ring to look like Saturn's rings.

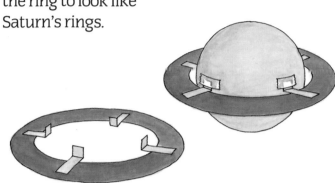

6 To attach the ring, make four 2-inch (5-cm) long cardboard tabs. Stick the tabs to the ring, fold them, and tape them to the planet, leaving a 1/2-inch 1-cm gap all around.

7 Wind some foil tape around a coat hanger. Tape different lengths of nylon thread to the planets and suspend them from the coat hanger.

The solar system

Our solar system contains nine planets orbiting the sun, which is our very own star.

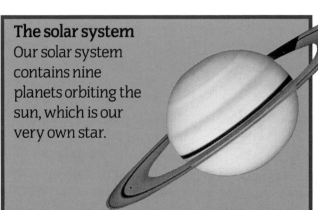

The four planets nearest to the sun – Mercury, Venus, Earth, and Mars – are small and rocky. Mercury is not much bigger than our moon. Venus is the hottest planet and has a heavy atmosphere with clouds of acid. Mars, sometimes called the "red planet," has ice caps at its north and south poles and four giant volcanoes. Next come four giant planets– Jupiter, Saturn, Uranus, and Neptune. Jupiter is big enough to hold 1,318 Earths! Saturn *(above)* is famous for its rings, which are made up of small pieces of rock and ice in orbit. Jupiter, Uranus, and Neptune have thin rings too, but they are not so easily visible. Pluto is the smallest known planet, with a temperature of around -380°F (-220°C)!

Blast-off!

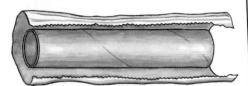

1 First cover a paper towel tube with silver foil.

YOU WILL NEED:
- paper towel tube ✓ large sheet of black paper ✓ silver foil
- red, blue, and pink paper ✓ corrugated paper ✓ round lid
- gray and white tissue paper ✓ foil stars ✓ PVA glue ✓ oak tag
- silver poster paint ✓ Fun-Tak ✓ pencil ✓ ruler ✓ scissors
- transparent tape ✓ brushes (for glue and paint)

2 Make a cone by drawing a circle about 4 inches (10 cm) in diameter on some oak tag. Cut out the circle, and then cut a slit from the edge to the center. Overlap the edges so that the cone fits on top of the tube and tape the edges together. Cover the cone in silver foil and then glue it on top of the tube.

3 Cut out three corrugated paper fins and paint them silver. Stick the fins to the sides of the rocket.

4 For the rocket's exhaust, cut strips of red, blue, and pink paper and glue them inside the bottom of the tube.

5 Position it against the black paper so your rocket will look like it's in space, and glue it on with PVA glue.

Rockets

Rockets launch spacecraft and satellites into space. They work just like firework rockets. Fuel burns inside, sending hot gases out at the back and pushing the rocket forward. Space rockets burn enormous amounts of fuel very quickly. They usually have two or three stages, which are really separate rockets stacked on top of each other. Each stage drops away when its fuel is used up. Spacecraft need such powerful rockets because they have to reach a speed of over 25,000 miles (40,000 km) an hour to escape from Earth's gravity. This is 40 times faster than a jet plane! Most rockets carrying spacecraft, probes, or satellites, including the space shuttle, are launched from the ground straight up into the sky. But in 1993, a Brazilian rocket was launched from an American plane about 9 miles (14 km) above the earth. The rocket carried a satellite designed to study the Amazonian rain forest.

6 Decorate your space background with shiny foil stars. Then scrunch small pieces of white and gray tissue paper into balls and glue them into a round lid. Glue this onto your space background.

Now you can put your rocket picture up on the wall with Fun-Tak......
3 — 2 — 1 — lift off!

Moonscape

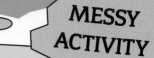

The moon is pitted with craters and covered with rocks and dust. The dark patches are flat plains called seas, but there is no water on the moon.

YOU WILL NEED:
- *9 oz (250 g) plain white flour* *4 1/2 oz (125 g) salt*
- *2 tablespoons of cooking oil* *water* *felt-tip pens*
- *brown, white, and black ready-mixed paints* *white oak tag*
- *toothpicks* *two small matchboxes* *craft knife* *Styrofoam*
- *toothpaste caps* *cookie sheet* *silver foil* *glue* *bowl*
- *egg carton* *cardboard base* *bendable straws* *scissors*
- *strong glue (UHU)* *modeling clay* *spoon* *fork*
- *brushes (for glue and paint)* *transparent tape*
- *cutting board*

1 Mix the flour and salt in a bowl. Then add the oil and enough water to make a non-sticky mixture. Knead well with your hands.

2 Mold the dough to make a lunar surface. Shape mountains and craters, and use a fork and spoon to create surface texture — you could even make some astronauts' footprints.

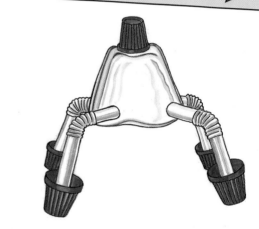

3 Line a cookie sheet with foil and bake your moonscape on the lower rack of the oven at 350°F (180°C/Gas 4) for about 30 minutes. When it has cooled, put it on a cardboard base and paint it.

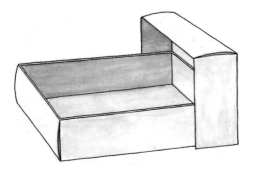

4 The astronauts arrived in a lunar module. Cover an egg carton cup with silver foil and stick a toothpaste cap on top. Attach four bendable straw legs to the cup with strong glue. The legs are held in toothpaste-cap feet with clay.

5 Astronauts traveled on the moon in a lunar rover. Use the bottom half of a matchbox for the rover's body. Cut the other matchbox in half and stick the two boxes together as shown.

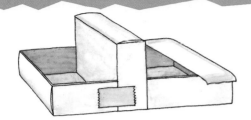

6 Tape the remaining half to the back for the astronauts' tools. Then cut a 1/2 inch (1-cm) wide strip of oak tag and glue it across the front of the rover. Cover the rover with silver foil.

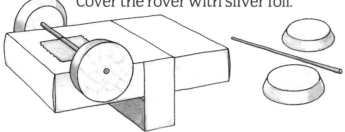

7 Ask an adult to help you cut out four Styrofoam wheels about 2 inches (4 cm) in diameter. Use two toothpicks for axles and tape the wheels to the bottom of the matchboxes.

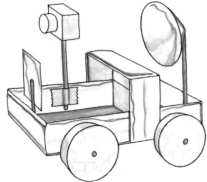

Man on the Moon

The moon is Earth's partner in space. Only 240,000 miles (384,000 km) away, the moon is about one-quarter the size of Earth. It is the only planet people have visited in space. American astronauts made six landings on the moon between 1969 and 1972. Because there is no weather on the moon, its surface hardly changes. If you went there today, you could see the astronauts' footprints as if they were made yesterday. Neil Armstrong was the first man to set foot on the moon. He traveled with two others in an Apollo spacecraft launched by a huge Saturn rocket. The journey took three days, and he and Edwin Aldrin landed on the moon's surface in a lunar module. They spent over two hours collecting rocks and setting up instruments. They were the first people ever to leave Earth to visit its satellite. Later astronauts took a lunar rover with them to the moon.

8 Make an oak tag instrument panel, long-range antenna, and Styrofoam camera. Glue this equipment to toothpicks taped to the rover.

Don't forget to plant a flag before returning to Earth.

Star Mural

1 The size of your star mural will depend on the available wall space. Tape a number of sheets of black paper together for the background of your mural.

2 Cut out 152 round shapes from the silver foil for ordinary stars. Then cut out seven star shapes from gold foil for very bright stars. These stars will make up 17 well-known constellations.

3 Glue the foil stars onto the black paper to create the constellations.

1. Draco, the Dragon, 2. Ursa Major, the Great Bear, 3. Cancer, the Crab, 4. Leo, the Lion, 5. Virgo, the Virgin, 6. Libra, the Scales, 7. Scorpius, the Scorpion, 8. Sagittarius, the Archer, 9. Lyra, the Lyre, 10. Aquila, the Eagle, 11. Capricornus, the Goat, 12. Aquarius, the Water Carrier 13. Pisces, the Fishes, 14. Aries, the Ram, 15. Taurus, the Bull, 16. Orion, the Hunter, 17. Gemini, the Twins.

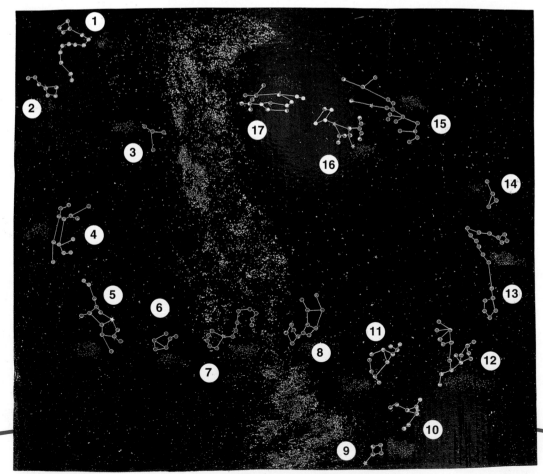

4 Join the stars together with white crayon to define the constellation shapes.

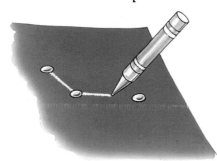

5 Brush some PVA glue onto the background and sprinkle on some glitter to create a sparkling Milky Way. Shake off any unwanted glitter.

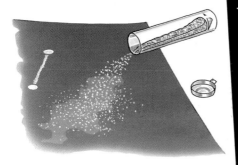

6 Stick your star mural up on the wall with Fun-Tak. Then look up at the night sky. Can you recognize any of the constellations? You may also see a hazy river of milky light stretching across the sky. If so, you are looking toward the heart of our galaxy, the Milky Way.

Constellations

Each of the stars that shines in the night sky is like our sun — an enormous, very hot ball of gas. Because they are so far away, the stars look like pinpoints of light. On a clear night there are so many that it is difficult to tell them apart. To help solve this problem, ancient astronomers joined stars together to make pictures. It was easy to remember the pictures and so recognize the stars. They often drew animals and people from legends. Ursa Major is the Great Bear; Leo, the Lion; and Orion is a Greek giant hunter. There are 88 constellations altogether. Most of the stars in the Great Bear are quite faint, but the seven brightest are arranged in a pattern known as the Big Dipper. Four of the stars form the cup (or the bear's bottom!), and the other three make a handle (or the bear's tail).

Friendly Aliens

MESSY ACTIVITY

YOU WILL NEED:
- wiffle ball ✓ poster paint ✓ chocolate-box tray ✓ egg carton
- small plastic flowerpot ✓ oak tag ✓ silver foil ✓ tissue paper
- foam pieces ✓ 2 screws ✓ string ✓ black trash can liner
- foil dish ✓ scissors ✓ toothpicks ✓ needle ✓ straws
- strong glue (UHU) ✓ transparent tape ✓ nylon thread
- Fun-Tak

1 Alien I's body is a wiffle ball. Tie a long piece of string around two of the holes.

2 For the eyes, cut out two segments from a chocolate-box tray. Scrunch up some silver foil into a small ball to make pupils, and stick them into the eyes. Then glue the eyes to the ball.

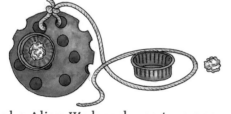

3 This strange creature has eight legs. Cut some straws into 4-inch 10-cm long pieces, and push the legs into holes in the ball.

4 To make Alien II's head, use two egg carton segments for eyes. Glue screws into them, and put a lump of Fun-Tak over the points. Tape the eyes together and onto a small flowerpot. Cut strips of silver foil and tissue paper for Alien II's brain. Tape and glue the strips to the inside of the pot.

5 Cut and bend a foil dish so that it fits onto the flowerpot. Twist some of the cut-off foil to make tentacles. Cut out two oak tag disks and push toothpicks through the middle and into the tentacle. Secure with tape. Then tape the tentacles to the front of the foil top.

6 Alien II is assembled with two pieces of string. One piece goes through the flowerpot and a hole in the foil dish. Cut a square from a black trash can liner and knot it to the string at the bottom of the flowerpot. Tape the other piece of string to the top half. Pull it and the top half will shoot up. Pull the other string and Alien II will swing, spin, and fly.

7 To make Alien III, paint foam pieces with poster paint. When they are dry, thread them onto pieces of nylon thread. For the head, accordion-fold a piece of oak tag and glue an oak tag disk to the front. Glue the head to the body. This crazy space crawler is controlled by three pieces of nylon thread attached to the head, body, and tail segments.

Alien life

Is there any form of life out in space? Years ago, people thought there might be life on Mars. But unmanned spacecraft landed there in 1976 and found nothing. In 1983, a Pioneer probe left the solar system, carrying a message from Earth. Astronomers are also trying to pick up radio signals from space, but so far no messages have been received. Radio signals are also sent from Earth, but since the next nearest star is over 250,000 times farther away than the sun, it will be a very long time before we receive a reply!

Some people think that we are already being visited by aliens. They point to sightings of objects in the sky known as Unidentified Flying Objects, or UFOs. Most of these turn out to be natural or man-made objects such as clouds or satellites. As yet we are no nearer to finding other forms of life.

Space shuttle

1 Remove any labels from the bottle by soaking it in warm water. To make the shuttle's underside and wings, place the bottle in the middle of a piece of white oak tag 14 x 9 inches (36 x 24 cm). Draw one wing shape and the underside, as shown. Then fold the oak tag in half and cut along the pencil line. Tape the underside to the bottle with strips of transparent tape.

> **MESSY ACTIVITY**
>
> YOU WILL NEED:
> - large plastic bottle ✔2 yogurt containers
> - glue ✔white oak tag ✔black poster paint
> - silver foil ✔pencil ✔scissors ✔ruler
> - transparent tape ✔compass
> - brushes (for glue and paint) ✔white acrylic paint (or poster paint and dishwashing liquid)
> - red tissue paper

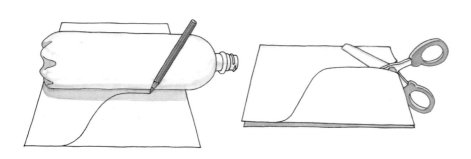

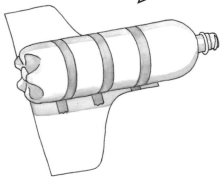

2 Draw a tail onto a piece of oak tag 6 x 4 inches (15 x 10 cm) and cut it out. Make a $\frac{1}{2}$-inch (1-cm) fold along the base of the tail, and tape it to the shuttle.

3 Tape the yogurt container engines into position.

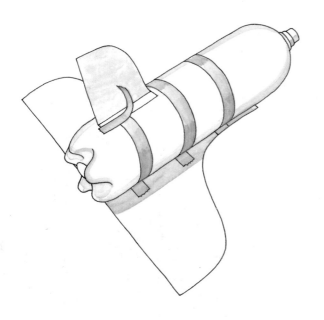

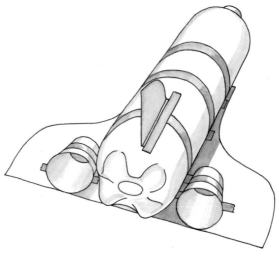

22

4 Make the nose cone by drawing a circle about 9 inches (22 cm) in diameter on some oak tag. Cut out the circle and then cut a segment from it as shown. Form the circle into a cone to fit around the bottle top. Secure it with tape.

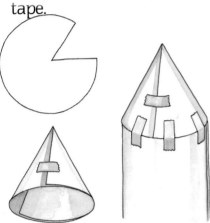

5 Paint the shuttle white. Use acrylic paint for all the plastic surfaces. (Poster paint will also stick to plastic and tape if mixed with a few drops of dishwashing liquid.) When the white paint is dry, paint the windows and underside black. Decorate your shuttle with silver foil markings. Use red tissue paper for the shuttle's exhaust.

Now your space shuttle can take off and land many times — it's a reusable spacecraft!

The American shuttle program

Rockets and spacecraft are very expensive to build, and before 1981 they were made to be used only once. In that year the first space shuttle, *Columbia*, spent more than 50 hours in space and then made a perfect landing back on Earth. The shuttle is a reusable spacecraft. It takes off upward, launched by two booster rockets that get used up in two minutes. These rockets then parachute down to the sea, to be used again for another flight. The huge fuel tank powers the shuttle's engines, and then it, too, falls away. The main part of the shuttle, called the orbiter, can carry up to seven astronauts, as well as a cargo of satellites and other items. After its space flight, the orbiter glides down through the atmosphere and lands like an aircraft on a long runway.

Space Station Control

Work on board your own space station.

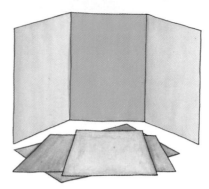

1 Cut off the top, bottom, and one side of a large cardboard box, leaving just three sides. These will form your control room. Paint or cover the cardboard.

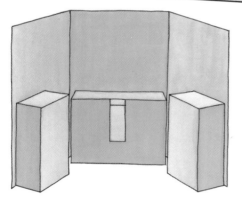

2 Use shoe boxes and small cardboard boxes to make the computers and control panels. Cover the boxes with blue paper or paint them with ready-mixed paint. Glue them along the bottom, the top, and sides of the control room.

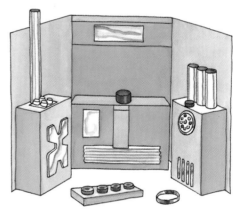

3 For instrument panels, use strong glue to attach bottle tops and lids to the top and sides of the control boxes. Foil dishes and tubes covered with silver foil make good space equipment. Paint popsicle sticks and Styrofoam packing with silver paint.

4 Paint space-age graphics on black paper to make a computer screen.

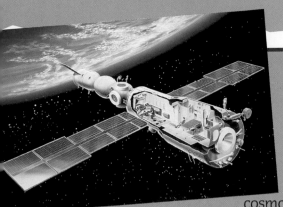

Space stations

A space station orbiting the earth is a place for astronauts and scientists to live and work. It must hold everything people need to stay alive. All their air, food, and water must be taken up from Earth. The main part of the Russian space station Mir (left), was launched in 1986, and orbited the Earth for 15 years. During that time the cosmonauts (Russian astronauts) ate, slept, washed, and exercised in the main part, powered by solar panels that turned sunlight into electricity. In later years further modules with laboratories and other equipment were added. The cosmonauts traveled to Mir by a Soyuz spacecraft, which remained docked to the space station until they returned to Earth. In 1995, U.S. astronaut Norman Thagard joined a mission to Mir and returned to Earth on the NASA space shuttle, which docked with Mir.

5 Put graphs and charts on the control room walls. Use paper fasteners for dials. Twisted wire and drinking straws make good antennas. Make a row of flashing control buttons using bottle tops covered with colored foil.

6 Your space station control is now complete. Of course, you could make a really big space station with lots of modules. All you have to do is add more cardboard boxes and equip them with space gadgets.

Exploring the Universe

Take a trip to the outer planets and beyond the solar system with your own board game.

YOU WILL NEED:
- black cardboard, white cardboard, and white oak tag (about 25 x 15 inches [60 x 40 cm])
- blue, gray, yellow, and orange paint
- PVA glue
- black marker pen
- pencil
- scissors
- brushes (for glue and paint)
- die
- crayons or felt-tip pens
- tracing paper

1 Use a piece of black cardboard for the game board.

2 Draw a round pathway about $1\frac{1}{2}$ inches (4 cm) wide on a large sheet of white oak tag, to look something like the shape shown here.

3 Mark the pathway into 80 playing squares. You start and finish on the first square, labeled Earth, and make a round journey clockwise. Cut out the pathway and glue it to the board. Then decorate the board with space drawings.

4 Paint the planet squares blue, the moons gray, the star yellow, and the galaxies orange. Use the picture as a guide to write each one's name in its space in order on the pathway.

Earth (planet); Moon (moon of Earth); Jupiter (planet); Titan (moon of Saturn); Uranus, Pluto (planets); Proxima Centauri (star); Small Magellanic Cloud, Leo I, Ursa Major, IC 1613; Large Magellanic Cloud, Leo II (galaxies); Neptune, Saturn (planets); Ganymede (moon of Jupiter); Mars (planet).

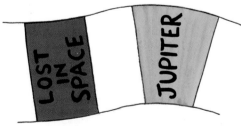

5 There are five "lost in space" and two "asteroids" squares. Color all of these black.

6 Make a small spaceship counter for each player. Trace this spaceship onto some cardboard and cut it out. Make each one a different color. Now find yourself a die and get ready to voyage into space!

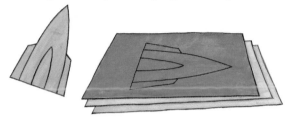

Rules of the game:

Each player starts on Earth and moves the number of spaces thrown on the die. Each time you land on a planet, moon, star, or galaxy you can have another throw of the die, or free turn. When you land on an "asteroids" or a "lost in space" square, you must miss a turn. If you land on an ordinary, unmarked square, you just wait for your next turn. The first voyager to complete the trip and land with the exact number back on Earth is the winner.

The universe

Even with the most powerful telescope, we can see only a small part of the universe. But stars and other objects in space also give off radio waves, and these can be "seen" by special telescopes. The largest single radio telescope dish in the world is at Arecibo, Puerto Rico. Its 1,000-feet (305-m) dish picks up radio signals from all over the sky. These signals help us to understand the universe and how it began. Most scientists think that the universe came into being about 15,000 million years ago. According to their theory, it began as one small lump. Then a massive explosion, known as the "Big Bang," blew material outward. Gas and dust formed after the explosion and created galaxies. These galaxies moved outward, and scientists believe that they are still doing so.

The Solar System

The Sun
The Sun is an enormous ball of gas. Its diameter is 109 times bigger than the Earth's. The Sun's center is extremely hot, about 25,000,000°F. As the Earth and the other planets in the solar system circle the Sun, they receive some of its light and heat. Light from the sun takes about 2 minutes to reach Mercury and 8 minutes to reach Earth. It takes over 5 hours to reach Pluto!

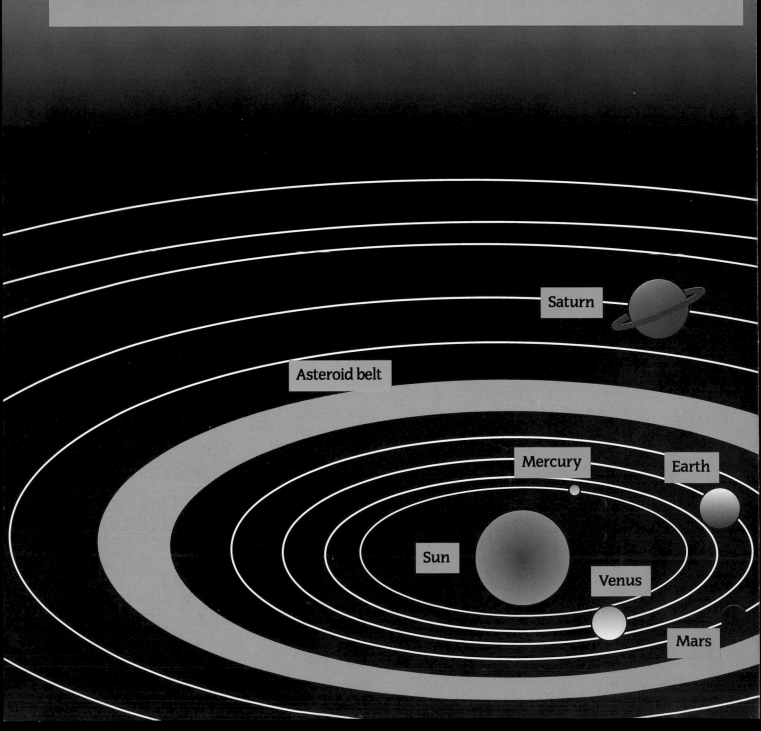

Saturn

Asteroid belt

Mercury

Earth

Sun

Venus

Mars

PLANET	distance from Sun in millions of miles	orbit (time taken to go around the sun in days or years)	diameter in miles	number of moons/satellites
Mercury	36	88 days	3,040	0
Venus	67	225 days	7,565	0
Earth	93	365 days	7,970	1
Mars	142	1.9 years	4,240	2
Jupiter	486	11.9 years	89,240	16+
Saturn	890	29.5 years	75,000	20+
Uranus	1,790	84.0 years	31,750	15+
Neptune	2,800	164.8 years	30,375	8
Pluto	3,690	247.7 years	1,875	1

Pluto

Neptune

Uranus

Jupiter

The Galaxy
Our Sun and solar system are in the Milky Way galaxy.
The Milky Way is a spiral galaxy. It is like a large ball with a flat disc across the middle. The Sun is in the disk, near the outer edge of the galaxy, about 143,000 billion million miles from the center!

Glossary

alien - a being from another world.

asteroid - a miniature planet that moves around the sun. There are thousands of asteroids between the orbits of Mars and Jupiter.

astronaut - a traveler in space; a spaceman or spacewoman.

astronomer - a scientist who studies the universe.

atmosphere - an envelope of gas surrounding a planet, such as the layer of air around the earth.

Big Bang - according to a scientific theory, the explosion that created the universe.

carbon dioxide - a gas. It forms much of the atmospheres of Mars and Venus, and is part of the atmosphere of Earth.

constellation - groups of stars named by ancient astronomers after legendary animals, people, and objects.

cosmonaut - a Russian astronaut.

Earth - the planet on which we live.

galaxy - a vast system of stars held together by gravity. Our solar system is in the Milky Way galaxy.

gravity - an invisible force that pulls everything down toward the center of a planet such as Earth; holds star systems together in a galaxy.

lunar module - a small craft used to carry astronauts from an Apollo spacecraft to the surface of the moon and back again.

Manned Maneuvering Unit (MMU) - a special backpack that allows an astronaut to move through space near a spacecraft.

Milky Way - the galaxy of stars to which our sun and the solar system belong.

module - a self-contained unit.

nuclear radiation - nuclear particles that are harmful to human beings.

orbit - the curved path followed by a planet around a star or by a satellite around a planet.

orbiter - the spacecraft of a space shuttle in which astronauts live and work.

planet - a ball of rock, metal, or gas revolving around a star. There are nine planets revolving around the sun, including Earth.

radio telescope - an instrument that picks up radio waves from space.

rocket - a powerful vehicle that blasts off from Earth to carry spacecraft into space.

satellite - [1] a man-made device sent into space to send information back to Earth; [2] a moon that orbits a planet (the moon is a satellite of the earth), or a planet that orbits a star (the earth is a satellite of the sun).

solar system - the sun and the planets revolving around it.

space - the unlimited expanse between all the planets, stars, and galaxies in the universe.

space shuttle - a reusable spacecraft that carries people and equipment.

space station - a large spacecraft that orbits the earth and acts as a home in space for astronauts and scientists.

star - an enormous, hot ball of gas, such as our sun. Stars look like points of light in the night sky because they are so far away.

sun - the star that gives heat and light to Earth and the other planets in the solar system. It is an enormous, very hot ball of gas.

Unidentified Flying Object (UFO) - something seen in the sky and thought to be a spacecraft from another world; sometimes called a "flying saucer."

universe - the whole of space and all the planets, stars, and galaxies in it.

Books to read

DK Readers: Rockets and Spaceships
ed. Linda Martin
(New York: DK Children, 2001)

If You Decide to Go to the Moon
by Faith McNulty
(New York: Scholastic, 2005)

The Planets in Our Solar System
by Franklyn M. Branley
(New York: HarperTrophy: 1998)

Roaring Rockets (Amazing Machines)
by Tony Mitton
(New York: Kingfisher, 2000)

Places to visit/Websites

New York Hall of Science
47-01 111th Street
Flushing Meadows
Corona Park
Queens, NY 11368
(718) 699-0005
Website: www.nyhallsci.org

Museum of Science and Space
Transit Planetarium
3280 S. Miami Avenue
Miami, Florida 33129
(305) 646-4200
Website: www.miamisci.org

Spaceport USA
Kennedy Space Center
Cape Canaveral
Florida 32899
(321) 452-2121
Website: www.spaceportusa.com

National Aeronautics
and Space Adminstration
Langley Research Center
Hampton, Virginia 23665
(757) 864-1000
Website: www.nasa.gov/centers
/langley/home/index.html

National Space Society
922 Pennsylvania Ave SE
Washington, D.C. 20003
(202) 429-1600
Email: nsshq@nss.org
Website: www.nss.org

Website

John F. Kennedy Space Center
Website: www.nasa.gov/centers
/kennedy/home/index.html

Index

Additional Photographs:

Dr. Seth Shostak/Science Photo Library 27;
Ducros/Jerrican/Science Photo Library 25; Earth
Satellite Corporation/Science Photo Library 7;
John Sanford & David Parker/Science Photo
Library 19; NASA/Science Photo Library 3, 9, 11,
13, 15, 17, 23; Zefa 21.